DARING TO *Love*

Opening the Door to Healing and Transformation
Workbook

*Companion or Standalone to the book
Daring To Love*

*Opening The Door to Healing
and Transformation*

T. NECHELLE

wordeee
where words connect
New York

DARING TO *Love*

Opening the Door to Healing and Transformation
WORKBOOK

*Companion or Standalone to the book
Daring To Love
Opening The Door to Healing
and Transformation*

T. NECHELLE

Daring To Love Opening the Door to Healing and Transformation Workbook

All rights reserved. No part of this book may be used or reproduced in any manner whatsoever in without the copyright owner's written permission except for the use of quotations book reviews.

Copyright © 2020 by T. Nechelle
First edition January 2021

Author Photograph: Jordan Medina
Cover Design: Omomato
Interior Design: Amit Dey

ISBN: 978-1-946274-57-1 (Paperback)
ISBN: 978-1-946274-58-8 (ebook)
LCCN: 2021900664

Published by Wordeee Beacon, NY
Website: www.wordeee.com
Twitter: wordeeeupdates
Facebook: wordeee
E-mail: contact@wordeee.com

Table of Contents

Introduction vii
Chapter 1 Pain 1
Chapter 2 Finding Your Truth 13
Chapter 3 Grace. 19
Chapter 4 Damage 23
Chapter 5 Honesty and Dignity 29
Chapter 6 Excuses. 33
Chapter 7 Determination 39
Chapter 8 Unconditional Love 43
Chapter 9 Revenge 47
Chapter 10 Moment of Reckoning 51
Chapter 11 Running 55
Chapter 12 Betrayal 59
Chapter 13 Love Never Fails 63
Chapter 14 Surrender. 67
Chapter 15 Love, Safety, and Security. 71

Introduction

This workbook is a companion or standalone workbook to *Daring to Love: Opening the Door to Healing and Transformation*.

Constructed to take you through the powerful process of unveiling shields of the heart that may be blocking your ability to love "full out," it will help you shift paradigms and unravel mindsets that no longer serve you or your relationships. As you review the questions and write your responses, you will notice that each set of questions builds upon the previous sets, increasing their effectiveness. If your answers require more space than is provided in the lined sections, write them on additional sheets of paper.

At the close of many of the Lessons and Exercises, you will find the word Actions. Actions words describe the instruction and the points of light to follow for your continuous improvement. To effectively use this workbook, you must be ready to be 100% honest with yourself and know you are a work in progress. Accept your truth and forgive yourself for holding your heart hostage.

Love of self is the purest form of love that one can express. It's now time to remove every self-made veil and label and be ready to have fierce "confrontational" conversations necessary to uncover the hidden greatness inside you...now and forever.... Are you ready to dare to love you first?

Chapter One

Pain

Lesson and Exercise

Understanding your pain and where it comes from is the key to healing. Pain comes in all forms, some of which are listed below. When the root of the pain is not examined and neutralized, it grows in our hearts, in our minds, and can destroy almost every relationship we have. Sometimes we are unaware of how our pain is manifesting itself, and we keep repeating the same mistakes over and over again, getting the same dysfunctional results. What pain are you holding onto today that does not allow you to become the best version of yourself? Are they real or perceived?

*Remember that **FEAR** can be described as False Evidence Appearing Real.*

Points of Pain

Questions:

Answer each question below by writing truthful answers.

Shaming: Think about one moment when you felt utterly ashamed.

1. How did you feel?

_____
_____
_____
_____
_____

2. How did you react?

_____
_____
_____
_____
_____

3. Why do you think you choose that reaction to deal with the shame you felt?

_____
_____
_____
_____
_____

4. Have you resolved the shame? If yes, awesome! If not, how will you begin the process of stepping away from the darkness of shame and into your light of authenticity?

_____
_____
_____
_____
_____

Keeping Secrets: Secrets can hurt.

1. Did you grow up in a household where the motto was, "What happens here, stay here?" If yes, what was something that you were unable to share outside of your house?

_____
_____
_____
_____
_____

2. What secrets are you keeping that may be manifesting in the form of physical, spiritual or psychological limitations in your life? Was it physical violence, emotional abuse, financial abuse, verbal abuse, or sexual abuse?

_____
_____
_____
_____
_____

3. Are you a victim of domestic abuse or any form of physical violence? If yes, what happened? You may consider this a purging session to get it out of your mind and spirit.

_____
_____
_____
_____
_____

Self-Esteem Erosion:

1. Do you think you may have a self-esteem issue? Are you intimated by others or wish you could be as bold as other people? If yes, identify that moments when you felt insecure?

_____
_____
_____
_____
_____

2. Why do you think this situation made you feel insecure?

_____
_____
_____
_____
_____

3. What have you done to strengthen your self-esteem? (Affirmations)

4. What are your small, successful accomplishments that you can build on to bolster your self-esteem? Examples: Finished school; got a promotion; completed a goal you set for yourself.

SUPPORT

1. Do you have one person in your life that you can trust?

2. Have you ever thought of seeing a psychologist/psychiatrist to help deal with the anxieties caused by secrets?

_____
_____
_____
_____
_____
_____

3. Have you ever been diagnosed with Post Traumatic Stress Disorder (PTSD)?

_____
_____
_____
_____
_____
_____

4. Do you have a Spiritual relationship with your higher power? Do you pray or meditate? If yes, does this benefit your life and in what ways? If not, would you be open to meditating?

_____
_____
_____
_____
_____
_____

5. Do you have a support system of family or friends who help you cope with difficult matters? If yes, great. If no, what resources can you identify to help you in the area you most need help? Research those resources and write down their names and contact numbers

_____

_____

_____

_____

_____

6. Describe how giving up your personal power empowered your abuser.

_____

_____

_____

_____

_____

7. If you are still in an abusive situation, do you have an exit strategy to keep you and/or your children safe? Start thinking about your emergency exit plan? If you don't know what to do, contact your local Domestic Violence community and ask them to help you develop a safe exit strategy. Write the phone number of the Domestic Violence resource center below.

_____

_____

_____

_____

_____

8. Do you self-sabotage because of fear? If yes, describe a situation where you know you created an unfavorable situation to end it before someone else did?

_____
_____
_____
_____
_____
_____
_____

9. Setting boundaries: Do you set boundaries in your relationship to ensure that you are not getting overwhelmed? Describe below some of the boundaries you have set to keep your state of peace. If you have not set boundaries, this is the perfect time to start thinking about doing so. Write them down now.

_____
_____
_____
_____
_____
_____
_____
_____
_____

10. Remember, you teach people how to treat you. Recognizing your patterns: Are there any patterns you see in your relationships? Describe the pattern below. What new pattern would you like to set?

_____
_____
_____
_____
_____

11. The way children interpret experience can affect their lives forever. If you have children, do you know your child's love language? Describe how you can reinforce their love language.

_____
_____
_____
_____
_____

12. Describe the lens your child is looking through as a witness in dysfunctional situations. How can a change in environment can support behaviors to shift it to a positive view?

_____
_____
_____
_____
_____

Actions:

Begin self–work with forgiveness. Look in the mirror every day and tell yourself three things that you love about YOU. Begin to become aware of your thoughts, i.e., mindfulness. Monitor self-talk and immediately stop any negative conversations. Replace with positive messages that re-affirm your true identity. Say to yourself, "I am worthy; I am able; I am awesome; I am first and not last; I am the head and not the tail; I will lend and not borrow; Financial doors are open for me."

Notes

Chapter Two

Finding Your Truth

Lesson and Exercises

Finding Your Truth

Not living in your truth or facing reality head-on can lead to many dysfunctions. I have learned that the truth will always reveal itself. No matter the length of time, five years or twenty, the light will shine on darkness. Although facing reality can be difficult, it will ultimately be the best choice. Honest communication allows you to keep your dignity. Remember, you are not responsible for the response or coping abilities of another person. When you are not honest with yourself, you ultimately are giving your power away. There are consequences to dishonesty, feelings of guilt and shame that can begin to fester inside you for way too long. Some of the questions might trigger other questions, write them down and give them attention. You have thought about them for a reason.

Questions:

Answer each question below with truthful answers.

1. What consequences have you experienced by not facing your truth? Describe the situation.

   _____
   _____
   _____
   _____
   _____

2. How do you cope with a reality you'd rather not have had? Circle the answer that best describes your "go-to" coping reflex.

   a. Destruction?

   b. Compartmentalization?

   c. Disillusionment?

   d. Superficiality?

   e. Armoring up?

3. What choices have you made to assist you in coming face-to-face with your authentic self? For example, meditation, spiritual empowerment, healing with dignity?

   _____
   _____
   _____
   _____
   _____

4. What do you value most? Your relationships, health, work ethic, your job, your peace of mind and why?

_____
_____
_____
_____
_____
_____

5. What principles guide you: values, integrity, equality, fairness, etc.?

_____
_____
_____
_____
_____
_____

6. What experiences bring you true joy (not what you think would make others happy)?

_____
_____
_____
_____
_____
_____

7. Who do you say you are?

_____
_____
_____
_____
_____
_____
_____

Actions:

Commit to one new positive habit every thirty days. By the end of the year, you will have developed twelve new habits that are getting you closer to the best version of yourself. Simultaneously, commit to breaking a negative habit that you know is not serving you. By the end of the year, you will have shifted your paradigm and be ready to love every part of your journey.

Notes

Daring to Love

Chapter Three

Grace

Lesson and Exercises

As I continue to share my struggles with secrets, shame, and lies in life, I am realizing more and more that each person has their own "Giant" to conquer. My encounters with all forms of abuse at the time felt unbearable but underneath the layers of basic survival was my innate ability to build my spiritual and resiliency muscles. My spirituality has allowed me to see God's Grace and Favor in my life. I can now view my universal brokenness as a beautiful reflection of compassion, empathy, and love. Brokenness is a universal language, I am not alone on this journey to find peace and joy, and neither are you.

You are not alone. When you come face-to-face with your denial, you will need tools to help you climb to the mountain of truth.

Questions:

Answer each question below by writing truthful answers.

1. What tools and/or resources do you have available to support you in the healing process? (e.g., accountability friends, professional help, revisiting childhood with family, trigger recognition, self-love practices).

_____

_____

_____

_____

_____

_____

_____

_____

_____

_____

Suggestions:

Professional help can help you uncover the shame, reveal the secrets, and discern what is real and what is false. It will provide tools for you to use as you struggle to cope. Revisit your childhood with your family. Unearth the secrets. Recognize your triggers and change what you are doing immediately—practice self-compassion. You didn't get here alone. Give yourself a break and treat yourself as gentle as the child that lives inside of you. Accept love and kindness. Don't shun it because you fear people may see behind your mask. Practice forgiveness.

Actions:

1. Meditate—As soon as you wake up, meditate for at least fifteen minutes daily to set the tone for the day. Vision in your mind that you will be having a productive, positive, fulfilling day.

2. Pray—Daily, pray for mutually beneficial reciprocated relationships and, of course, anything else you deem necessary. Pray, don't worry; Hope, don't doubt; Have faith over fear.

3. Go for a quiet walk—Declutter your mind. The peace and stillness of nature release positive neurological hormones in your brain.

4. Do something that gives you joy in your private time; play the piano, sing, paint, cook, read, or try something you've never done before. Life is too short not to try new and exciting things. Fall in love with yourself for the first time or renew your relationship with yourself.

Notes

Chapter Four

Damage

Lesson and Exercises

Damaged people can be lonely behind their masks. My body was the source of many cause and effect inflictions, leading to feelings of rejection and unworthiness. I set low expectations for others and, sadly, even lower expectations for myself to avoid disappointments. I would avoid loneliness at any cost. The disconnect between my spirit and body kept me in a divided state, completely out of line with my true self. Does this sound familiar?

Questions:
Answer each question below by writing truthful answers.

1. Are you afraid of being alone? If yes, why are you afraid to be alone?

___

___

___

___

___

2. Have you identified any areas of your life where you don't feel secure? If yes, write down what you think maybe the reason for your low self-esteem related to this issue?

_____
_____
_____
_____
_____
_____

3. Do you express frustration when it comes to a lack of control in the form of anger or aggression? If yes, do you know why that is your initial response?

_____
_____
_____
_____
_____
_____

4. Do you engage in any self-destructive behaviors, such as eating disorders, substance abuse or sexual promiscuity? If yes, do you recognize these behaviors as self-destructive?

_____
_____
_____
_____
_____
_____

Acknowledgment is the first step to overcoming any unwanted behavior:

5. Acknowledge that you are lonely. Is your feeling of loneliness situational or chronic? Describe times when you feel lonely.

   _____
   _____
   _____
   _____
   _____
   _____
   _____

6. Describe action steps you will take to combat loneliness.

   _____
   _____
   _____
   _____
   _____
   _____
   _____

Actions:

Potential solutions to help with feelings of loneliness:

   a. Call a friend that has known you for years.

   b. Change your situation. Watch a movie that makes you laugh, cook your favorite meal for dinner, write in your journal to get feelings out of your head.

   c. Exercise—Yoga, bike riding, brisk walking to get your blood pumping and your lungs filled with deep cleansing breaths.

d. Volunteer to help others in need, become a blessing. This will help strengthen your grateful muscles.

e. Consider professional help or counseling.

Notes

Daring to Love

Chapter Five

Honesty and Dignity

Lesson and Exercises

You may also be surprised to find that your honesty and your sense of dignity, knowing you handled the situation like the mature adult you claim to be, is a reward in itself. At the root of going backward is that we go back into defense mode and often lie to ourselves and others. Remember, dishonesty stops you from being the best version of yourself! Dishonesty brings about feelings of shame and guilt. The enemy is happy when you carry this around inside. Free yourself and stomp on the enemy's head by letting go of dishonesty!

Questions:
Answer each question below by writing truthful answers.

1. Are you holding on to a dysfunctional relationship when deep down, you know it needs to end? If yes, describe why you think you are not willing to let the relationship go.

_____
_____
_____
_____
_____

2. Are you able to be honest with yourself, even if you're not ready, to be honest with your partner? Describe what it will take to be honest with the person with whom you are in a relationship?

_____
_____
_____
_____
_____
_____

3. Do you think it's fair to just wait for something better to come along? If yes, describe how you would feel if your partner was doing that to you?

_____
_____
_____
_____
_____
_____

4. Write a personal commitment statement to honesty below. Example: I will no longer justifying dishonesty.

_____
_____
_____
_____
_____
_____

5. Write an agreement statement with yourself to be trustworthy and authentic.

6. Write each of the lies or false labels that you have told yourself in the past. Example: I will never find love.

7. Write the opposite of the lie or false label you wrote above.

8. Take a red pen and cross out the lies/false labels and only focus on the new truths about yourself. Read the truths you wrote about yourself out loud in a mirror every day.

Notes

Chapter Six

Excuses

Lesson and Exercises

"Excuses are the tools of the incompetent, used to build bridges to nowhere and monuments of nothingness."

—**President Barack Obama**

Remembering this pledge from my Temple University days pressed me to start moving toward a new mark. I began to realize that my current situation didn't define me. I was finished making permanent decisions to address my temporary circumstances. The abusers were being removed from my life one at a time, and I was no longer willing to be the biggest abuser of them all. However, in the transformation stage, you may try to run back to what you know—making excuses. Can you hear your own excuses coming a mile away?

Questions:

Answer each question below by writing truthful answers.

1. Describe your dominant mindset. Do you leave things up to chance or make no decisions when they need to be made?

   _____
   _____
   _____
   _____
   _____

2. Do you blame others for your mistakes or take ownership? Describe a time that you now realize you need to take ownership of the mistake that occurred.

   _____
   _____
   _____
   _____
   _____

3. Do you believe someone else is responsible for your life? Describe how you take responsibility for your life's blueprint.

   _____
   _____
   _____
   _____
   _____

4. Describe how complaining, criticizing, or whining has delayed your progress in life.

5. Describe a time you have given away your power.

6. Describe ways in which you can maintain your own personal power.

Action steps to own your power:

1. Stop comparing yourself to others. The truth is, other people are probably comparing themselves to you.

2. Stop fearing the unknown. Sure, things may go wrong.

3. Stop blaming others for your misfortune.

4. Take responsibility.

5. Take action.

6. Set small, attainable goals.

7. Learn from your mistakes.

8. Don't focus on your weaknesses. Focus on your strength.

9. Listen to motivational messages that empower your mind.

Notes

Daring to Love

Determination

Lesson and Exercises

Determination comes when your self-worth, value, and mental independence are nonnegotiable. You are proud of the decision you are making and you are seeing your goals coming to fruition. A focused mind is a powerful weapon; coupled with a never-quit fighter spirit is a recipe for becoming unstoppable. I learned to stop looking at my failures and started looking at my successes, no matter how big or small. Failure was not an option for me any longer. I would use my lessons in life as mountains to stand on versus valleys to stand in.

Questions:
Answer each question below by writing truthful answers.

1. Describe your definition of a successful life.

_____
_____
_____
_____
_____

2. Have you found your purpose in life? Circle one: Yes or No.

   a. Describe: What is your purpose in life.

   _____
   _____
   _____
   _____

   b. Describe what you dreamed of becoming as a child. Is your purpose in line with that original dream.

   _____
   _____
   _____
   _____

3. Do you have specific goals you want to accomplish? Describe what they are and what are the dates and times to achieve your goals.

   _____
   _____
   _____
   _____

Note: Don't be paralyzed by perfection. It has been said many times you don't have to be great to get started, but you have to get started to be great. Not trying because you fear failure will leave you stuck in the rat race of life.

Actions:

1. Tell yourself every day you will not settle for less in life. Remember: Do whatever it takes to succeed on your terms.

2. Make a specific goal, no matter how small and accomplish it. Start building on small goals.

3. Know, categorically, if a change is necessary. Only you can do it.

4. If you don't have the education to do what you want to do, go back to school.

5. Apply for that job whether you think you will get it or not.

6. Don't rely on others and find a way to be self-sufficient, no matter how humble the work may be.

7. Delay gratification.

8. Withstand the temptation to make excuses.

9. Focus.

10. Resolve old baggage. Just let it go.

11. Count your blessings...daily.

12. Reward yourself.

13. Be kind to yourself and others.

14. Write in your journal.

Notes

Chapter Eight

Unconditional Love

Lesson and Exercises

Unconditional love is probably the hardest thing to attain. We are, it seems, wired to be judgmental and ego-tripping. For the first time, I was receiving pure love. It didn't feel familiar. It felt euphoric. The magical feeling of love made my heart beat louder and my stomach turn in knots. Although love opened a new door in my heart, the old doors where unworthiness, doubt, jealousy and insecurity were housed had not fully been closed. I wasn't ready to believe genuine love could exist. Understanding that I, too, deserved unconditional love and support wasn't within my natural range of experiences.

Questions:

Answer each question below by writing truthful answers.

1. It has been said, "Love is blind." Describe a time when you were blinded by love.

_____
_____
_____
_____

2. Describe what unconditional love looks like to you.

_____
_____
_____
_____
_____
_____
_____

3. Do you believe romantic love can be unconditional?

_____
_____
_____
_____
_____
_____
_____

4. Describe a time when you were judgmental about love in your relationship or someone else's?

_____
_____
_____
_____
_____
_____
_____

5. Who have you ever loved unconditionally? Why did you love that person unconditionally? Describe how that unconditional love made you feel.

_____
_____
_____
_____
_____
_____
_____
_____

Actions:

1. Practice being vulnerable in your actions and communications.
2. Practice forgiveness. Remember, forgiveness is not for the other person. Forgiveness is for you so that bitterness doesn't creep into your heart. You are not perfect, either. As you attempt to hold on to grudges and are unforgiving, remember that about yourself.

Notes

Revenge

Lesson and Exercises

Feelings of resentment are often stimulated by the possibility of being rejected over and over again, too afraid to be vulnerable and too afraid to face the possibility of losing a love I never fully embraced. Revenge was the easiest way to exchange my hurt feelings for anger.

Questions:
Answer each question below by writing truthful answers.

1. Describe a situation where you were disappointed and how you handled the disappointment, abandonment, and/or fear?

---

2. Have you taken revenge on the person who hurt you? If so, describe what you did to vindicate yourself.

3. Describe how you could have handled the situation differently.

4. Did your revenge elicit revenge from the other person? If so, describe the cycle that occurred.

5. Describe how you will break the cycle.

_____
_____
_____
_____
_____
_____
_____

Actions:

1. Practice communicating your feelings. "I don't feel secure when you do this...."
2. Talk to someone before committing to any action of revenge. Have an accountability partner.
3. Create distance from any explosive situations.
4. If you fall backward, give yourself a break...practice self-compassion.
5. Ask for help. Become clear on your morals and values as they are right now.
6. Realize that the past is the past; pierce the veil.
7. Create a "re-do." Realize you did the best you could at the time.
8. Start acting in accordance with your new moral and value system. Talk honestly to yourself and others.
9. Identify your biggest regrets. Turn the page.
10. Tackle the big ones.
11. Consistently practice self-love. Give yourself some slack.
12. Keep finding ways to communicate with the person you hurt and yourself.

Notes

Chapter Ten

Moment of Reckoning

Lesson and Exercises

There are consequences to every action in life. Sabotaging my marriage was catapulted by a need to feel wanted and loved. I wanted a kind of love from my husband that I wasn't willing to give myself. Over the years, I had subconsciously programmed others how to treat me. I failed to set boundaries for myself or anyone else.

Questions:

Answer each question below truthfully.

1. Did you get married because of any of these reasons below? Circle which one is closest to the reason you got married or committed to a relationship.

    a. Two incomes. I couldn't make it on my own financially.

    b. Co-dependence. I can't live without this person; they complete me.

    c. Don't like to be alone.

    d. Abstaining from sex is too hard, and you don't want to feel guilting by fornicating.

e. Want to control someone.

f. Found my soul mate.

Actions:

1. Describe your belief about coupling. What does it mean to you?

2. Describe ways to practice finding your own space, interests, and hobbies apart from your partner's.

3. Describe the things you do/need from your partner that you can't get from your friends.

4. Describe things you want to change in your relationship.

Notes

Daring to Love

Running

Lesson and Exercises

Running
Running was a coping mechanism that I used to avoid facing pain directly. Instead of using my failures as an opportunity to grow, I used them to shrink and become invisible. Compartmentalizing pain never brings about resolution. It gives you a false sense of conquering the pain you did not have the courage to address. The sanctity of marriage deserves a fight response…not a flight response.

Questions:
Answer each question below by writing truthful answers.

1. Do you pack your entire day with activities to avoid facing your situation? If yes, why do you think you have adopted this coping mechanism?

_____
_____
_____
_____

2. Will you commit to removing your mask and standing in your truth? If yes, describe what standing in your truth means to you.

_____
_____
_____
_____
_____
_____
_____

3. Will you allow the people in your life to do the same? If yes, describe how you will give them this permission.

_____
_____
_____
_____
_____
_____
_____

Actions to live a positive life:

1. Meditate for 10 minutes before you get out of bed.
2. Set your day's intention daily.
3. Acknowledge your fear and take action to eliminate the old record playing over and over in your head.
4. Take time out with your partner and just be in their presence.
5. Share something about you with your partner they didn't know.
6. Practice trusting.

Notes

Betrayal

Lesson and Exercises

Betrayal
It would have been easy to displace my anger and blame someone else for my choices that caused chaos in my life. But displacement tactics strip ownership from the responsible party. I learned to embrace my exposure because it ultimately led to my freedom blessing.

Questions:
Answer each question below by writing truthful answers.

1. Have you experienced betrayal? If yes, describe how it has impacted you?

   _____
   _____
   _____
   _____
   _____

2. Are you in a social group that doesn't share your deepest values? Describe why you are associating with them.

___
___
___
___
___
___

3. Are you sharing the wrong information with your friends? Describe why you need to receive approval from the people around you.

___
___
___
___
___
___

4. Are you aware that a friend who enables you to do the wrong thing will do the wrong thing, too? Describe a situation where your friend helped you to do something that was not right.

___
___
___
___
___
___

5. Describe what boundaries you can set around your relationships.

_____
_____
_____
_____
_____
_____
_____

6. Do you recognize the role you play in your betrayal? Describe how you will take ownership of your actions.

_____
_____
_____
_____
_____
_____
_____

Actions:

1. If you are the origin of the drama, admit it. *Own* your drama.
2. Forgive the offending party but decide if they are worth your time.
3. Forgive completely but set boundaries.
4. Don't pressure yourself to, "Just let it go."
5. Don't rehash the past. Appreciate that, in time, why you MUST let it go.
6. Break down the wall that blocks communication.

Notes

Chapter Thirteen

Love Never Fails

Lesson and Exercises

Once I was finally able to forgive myself for accepting less than I deserved, I was able to find love, safety, and security inside my own heart. I had been so scared of love for most of my life, but love introduced me to freedom.

Questions:

Answer each question below by writing truthful answers.

1. Do you believe that loving with your full heart can give you freedom? Describe why you think love can or can't give you a sense of freedom.

   _____
   _____
   _____
   _____
   _____
   _____
   _____

2. Describe why you need to love from a space of freedom versus fear.

3. Do you have a strong relationship with your creator? If yes, describe what that loves feels like to you.

4. Do you believe that you can trust that, "True love never fails?" Describe why you do or don't believe this.

Actions:

1. What can you do every day to show your appreciation of love toward your partner?

2. Describe how you can show gratitude to your partner daily.

3. List what you are grateful for and state these things daily.

4. Pass it forward, so your children can break the cycle of dysfunctional love.

5. Strengthen your love by spending meaningful time together.

6. Strengthen your bond with your creator.

Note: Trust is oxygen for love. No trust, no love.

Notes

Chapter Fourteen

Surrender

Lesson and Exercises

Through my personal relationship with my God, I'm letting my light shine through to the world from the inside out. I continue to become freer with every step toward honesty and transparency about my feelings and about who I am today. This shift requires harmony between fortitude and vulnerability. Understanding the law of attraction, I am excited about giving my husband my all as our love is in constant motion of reciprocation.

Questions:
Answer each question below by writing truthful answers.

1. Describe what surrender means to you.

_____
_____
_____
_____
_____
_____
_____

2. Describe what is the worst thing that you think can happen if you surrender.

_____
_____
_____
_____
_____
_____
_____

3. Describe things that you believe are not acceptable in a relationship.

_____
_____
_____
_____
_____
_____
_____

Surrendering requires:

1. Problem-solving.
2. Releasing judgment and negativity.
3. Remaining in the present.
4. Transcending ego and subconscious programming.
5. Knowing your true self.
6. Facilitating positive changes in your relationship.

Actions:

1. Do exercises that will allow you to increase positive thoughts about yourself and your partner; Daily affirmations stating positive statements about yourself. For example, I am worthy. I am loved. I am beautiful. I am smart. I am enough. I am cherished. Think up your own affirmations.

2. Look in the mirror daily and tell yourself five things that you are proud of accomplishing in your life.

3. Look in the mirror and think of two things you can forgive yourself for today.

Remember these key things:

1. Better communication with yourself leads to better communication with your partner.

2. Start trusting yourself. Trust that you are enough. Trust your intuition. Trust your body. Trust in your ability to conquer your fears. Trust in yourself will help you to trust others. Trust will help you to be vulnerable.

3. Trust the one you love. Let God into your heart.

4. Describe a situation where you decided to trust in love more.

Notes

Chapter Fifteen

Love, Safety, and Security

Lesson and Exercises

Once I was finally able to forgive myself for accepting less than I deserved, I was able to find love, safety, and security inside my own heart. I had been scared of love for most of my life, but love introduced me to freedom.

Questions:

Answer each question below by writing truthful answers.

1. Describe how your relationship improved once you surrendered to love.

2. Describe how you have grown as a couple.

___

3. Describe how it feels to have your partner as your best friend.

___

Actions to think about :

1. Describe things you can do to deepen your and your partner's intimacy.

___

Suggestions for intimacy:

Have regular dating days and keep dating each other.

Go on vacation. Have second, third, fourth honeymoons when needed.

Have dedicated sacred spiritual time together.

Remember always to speak lovingly and kindly to each other.

Tell the truth even when it may be uncomfortable. Forgiveness is the most precious gift you can give to yourself and to the person you love.

Always remember:

"Love is patient, love is kind. It does not envy, it does not boast, it is not proud. It does not dishonor others, it is not self-seeking, it is not easily angered, it keeps no record of wrongs. Love does not delight in evil but rejoices with the truth. It always protects, always trusts, always hopes, always perseveres. Love never fails."

First Corinthians 13: 4-8

The goal of using the *Daring To Love Workbook* is to help you identify some of the areas in your life that may have held you back from daring to love. You are a work in progress that will continue to grow forever. You can use this book over and over again. Learning to love yourself and every aspect of your life's journey is truly the greatest gift of all. It is the very thing that makes you authentic. You have survived the storms of life. Now is the time for you to go forward and thrive. Let the world see you as a beautiful and uniquely designed rainbow that can brighten any cloudy day.

Notes

T. Nechelle

Daring to Love

T. Nechelle

Daring to Love

T. Nechelle

Daring to Love